STOUGHTON PUBLIC LIBRARY

3 1646 00152 9331

PUBLIC LIBRARY

D0810784

STOUGHTON PUBLIC LIBRARY
DISCARDED

DEMCO

MADELEINE ALBRIGHT

MADELEINE ALBRIGHT

She Speaks for America
by Suzanne Freedman

A Book Report Biography
FRANKLIN WATTS
A Division of Grolier Publishing
New York / London / Hong Kong / Sydney
Danbury, Connecticut

JB
Albright
Fre

frontispiece: Secretary-of-State-elect Madeleine Albright testifies
during her January 1997 confirmation hearings before the
Senate Foreign Relations Committee.

Photographs ©: AP/Wide World Photos: 2 (Joe Marquette), 71, 77; Archive
Photos: 27, 36; Chicago Sun Times: 47; Corbis-Bettmann: 66; Gamma-Liai-
son: 57, 90; Milan Jankovic 42, 33; Reuters/Archive Photos: 68, 22 (Win
McNamee); Reuters/Corbis-Bettmann: 14, 81; United Nations: 63 (M.
Grant), 17 (E. Schneider); UPI/Corbis-Bettmann: 37, 52, 54; 85; Wellesley
College Archives: 45.

Visit Franklin Watts on the Internet at:
http://publishing.grolier.com

Library of Congress
Cataloging-in-Publication Data

Freedman, Suzanne, 1932–
Madeleine Albright: she speaks for America / Suzanne Freedman.
    p. cm.—(Book report biography)
Includes bibliographical references (p.) and index.
Summary: Focuses on the career of the former United States ambas-
sador to the United Nations who became the first woman to serve as sec-
retary of state.
ISBN 0-531-11454-6
    1. Albright, Madeleine Korbel—Juvenile literature. 2. Women cabi-
net officers—United States— Biography—Juvenile literature. 3. Cabinet
officers—United States—Biography—Juvenile literature. 4. United
Nations—Officials and employees—Biography—Juvenile literature. 5.
Ambassadors—United States—Biography—Juvenile literature. [1. Albright, Madeleine Korbel. 2. Cabinet officers. 3. Ambassadors. 4. Women—
Biography.] I. Title II. Series.
    Q840.8.A37F74 1998
    327.73'0092—dc21
    [B]   97-13840
                                                                              CIP
                                                                               AC

© 1998 by Suzanne Freedman
All rights reserved. Published simultaneously in Canada
Printed in the United States of America
1 2 3 4 5 6 7 8 9 10 R 07 06 05 04 03 02 01 00 99 98

In the tradition of Madeleine Albright, women have dared to dream and then do what others said could not be done. Her courage, determination, discipline, and vision have changed women's lives. Madeleine Albright's dream has become a reality, and her example inspires us all.

I dedicate this book to the accomplished women in my family—Carole, Ellen, and Holly—and to my two young granddaughters, Sally and Hannah, whose dreams have a good chance of becoming reality and whose future will be filled with endless possibilities.

5/15/98 Pub.

CONTENTS

CHAPTER ONE

"SO HONORED AND SO PROUD"

After defeating George Bush in the 1992 presidential election, President-elect Bill Clinton faced many serious responsibilities, including the selection of a *cabinet*. The cabinet is the group of government officials—the heads, or secretaries, of the executive branch departments and other appointees—that gives advice to the president. Although Congress had originally created only three executive departments—state, war, and treasury—in 1789, by 1992 the number of executive departments had grown to 14. Like all presidents, Clinton had the constitutional authority to appoint the heads of these executive departments, but his appointees had to be confirmed by the U.S. Senate. Clinton vowed that his Cabinet would "look like America."

For his presidential campaign, Bill Clinton had hired a team of four advisers who had worked in the administration (1976–80) of President Jimmy Carter. These political veterans had developed campaign strategies that put Bush, the incumbent Republican president, on the defensive about his record in foreign affairs. Following his victory, Clinton wanted the four foreign-policy advisers to work in his administration. He picked Warren Christopher for the post of secretary of state; Anthony Lake as national security adviser; and Samuel Berger as deputy national security adviser. The fourth campaign adviser was Madeleine Albright.

Albright had considerable experience in government and politics. She had served as a staff member on Carter's *National Security Council*, the advisory group that makes recommendations to the president on matters involving national security. She had also been a foreign-policy adviser to three Democratic presidential hopefuls: Edmund Muskie, Walter Mondale, and Michael Dukakis. Albright's hard work as adviser to these important politicians had brought her to the attention of Clinton. The two had never really talked until the spring of 1992, when they met at the Democratic Governors Association annual dinner. They hit it off right away.

A few days after Clinton's victory, a member of his staff called Albright to ask whether she would be interested in the job of United States permanent representative to the United Nations (informally known as U.S. ambassador to the United Nations). If her answer was "yes," they wanted her to fly to Little Rock, Arkansas, at once. "It was a little sticky," said Albright, "because I was hosting a party the next evening, and they [Clinton's staff] told me not to tell anyone where I was going." Albright flew to Little Rock and had a long meeting with Clinton, who personally asked her to take the job. She accepted at once.

With her three daughters at her side the next day, Albright stood by Clinton as he told the world that she was his choice to be the U.S. ambassador to the UN. In his search for a qualified nominee, Clinton said that he had wanted someone who was tenacious, optimistic, and experienced in world affairs and that Albright satisfied all three requirements. Upon accepting the nomination, Albright

"You can . . . understand how proud I will be to sit at the United Nations behind the nameplate that says 'United States of America.'"

said, "I have to say it is a special personal honor for this American to be asked to serve. . . . You can . . . understand how proud I will be to sit at the United Nations behind the nameplate that says 'United States of America.'" If confirmed by the Senate, Madeleine Albright would become the

In December 1992, President-elect Bill Clinton answers questions during a press conference to introduce his cabinet nominees, including Madeleine Albright (second from the left).

21st U.S. ambassador since the UN was created in 1945 and the second woman to fill the post. Appointed by President Ronald Reagan in 1981, Jeane J. Kirkpatrick had served as ambassador to the UN for four years.

SENATE CONFIRMATION

In 1993, Senator Jesse Helms (R-North Carolina)* chaired the Senate Foreign Relations Committee, presiding over 17 members—a nearly equal mix of Republicans and Democrats. That committee has traditionally conducted *confirmation* hearings for the post of UN ambassador, and Albright would appear before it.

At her confirmation hearing on January 21, 1993, Madeleine Albright told the Senate Foreign Relations Committee that she would not have been in the United States had it not been for the United Nations. Her father, Josef Korbel, had been a Czechoslovakian diplomat and a member of a special UN commission in 1948. After a communist takeover in Czechoslovakia, he asked for and was granted *political asylum* in the United States. Albright said, "Thanks to the generosity of the American people," she and her family "had an opportunity to grow up as free Americans."

Albright went on to describe what she planned to accomplish in her role as U.S. ambassador to the UN:

> If confirmed, I intend to strengthen the ties between the United Nations and Congress

*Information in parentheses identifies the political party and home state of members of Congress.

by opening my offices in New York and Washington to you [and] by inviting as many of you as possible to New York, perhaps as delegates or to observe the work that is going on there. . . . I will always be the United States Ambassador to the United Nations and not the United Nations Ambassador to the United States.

After the committee met with Albright, it voted on a resolution recommending that she be confirmed. Accepting the committee's recommendation, the full Senate gave Albright unanimous voice approval.

Once she arrived at the United Nations in 1993, Albright was passionate about injustices and abuses overseas and enthusiastic about the role the United States should play in international wars, no matter how small. She testified tirelessly before congressional committees and frequently shared a platform with Senator Jesse Helms. A vocal critic of the United Nations, Helms called Albright a "tough and courageous lady."

For four years, Ambassador Albright participated in cabinet meetings and served on the National Security Council, helping to shape U.S. foreign policy. She was briefed, or given essential and often top-secret information, on national security issues, and other ambassadors viewed

*Ambassador Madeleine Albright speaks with
Ambassador Roble Olhaye of Djibouti at a 1994
UN Security Council meeting. As UN ambassador,
Albright emerged as a leading official in the
Clinton Administration.*

her as the U.S. president's personal representative to the UN. In turn, other governments knew that when they talked to her, their concerns were heard at the highest levels of the U.S. government. Because she dealt with more representatives of foreign nations each day than anyone else in the administration, Albright provided the president and his advisers with up-to-the-minute knowledge of what was happening at the United Nations and around the world. She was on the front lines of foreign policy every day and saw how people responded to U.S. foreign policy. Albright eventually emerged as one of the most outspoken and visible members of Clinton's foreign policy team and consistently pushed the White House toward forceful military responses.

ANOTHER CALL FROM THE PRESIDENT

Two days before the 1996 presidential election, Senator Patrick Leahy (D-Vermont) sat across from Ambassador Albright in the dining room of her Waldorf Towers suite, the official New York City residence of the UN ambassador. Secretary of State Warren Christopher had just told President Clinton privately that he wanted to retire from his post as secretary of state to rejoin his old law firm, O'Melveny and Myers, in Los Angeles, California. A *New York Times* reporter later asked Christopher what he would do there. "Try to stay off the airplane as much as possible—get my body . . . organized," Christopher replied with a smile. He was the most traveled secretary of state in U.S. history, having flown 765,000 miles during his time in office.

Somehow, Albright and her old friend Leahy knew about Christopher's plans. The senator began playing a "what-if" game. He asked Albright what she would do if she were to become secretary of state. Because Christopher had not officially announced his intentions, Leahy expected her to avoid the question. Albright, however, spent the next 20 minutes giving Leahy her world views, sounding as if she were rehearsing for another confirmation hearing.

On November 5, Bill Clinton defeated Republican challenger Bob Dole, becoming the first Democratic president to be reelected since Franklin D. Roosevelt in 1944. As his last official act, Warren Christopher would attend Clinton's second inauguration on January 20, 1997. Because the secretary of state is one of the most important officials in the federal government, finding a successor to Christopher was among Clinton's highest priorities in preparing for his second term. The secretary of state helps the president in many ways, including communicating with other countries on behalf of the United States, negotiating foreign treaties and agreements, and deciding the best way to deal with other countries.

Madeleine Albright was high up on Clinton's list of candidates for secretary of state. She had proven to be the administration's most skillful foreign policy salesperson during her four years at the United Nations. Clinton always said that Albright worked hard to make foreign policy look easy. Albright continued to tell reporters that she loved her job at the United Nations, but, from the beginning, she began consulting in private with her closest advisers on what her next step should be. At one point, she seriously considered a run for the Senate, but she quickly gave up that idea because she didn't have a home state to represent. (Her home was in Washington, D.C., which is not represented by a senator.)

Speculation continued to rise about Albright's replacing Christopher at the State Department. Responding to the rumors, Albright said, "The silver lining to the speculation is that people no longer think it's preposterous for there to be a woman Secretary of State." A Clinton confidant who was interviewing candidates warned Albright that aggressively seeking the job would backfire. So there wasn't much

> **"The silver lining to the speculation is that people no longer think it's preposterous for there to be a woman Secretary of State."**

Albright could do except hope her investments would pay off. She had won over many allies, including First Lady Hillary Clinton, who became Albright's greatest champion for the job. The two Wellesley graduates had always liked each other. Another important ally was her old friend Jesse Helms, the conservative chair of the Senate Foreign Relations Committee. There were, however, some opponents—including Treasury Secretary Robert Rubin, Chief of Staff Erskine Bowles, and Clinton confidante Vernon Jordan—who felt Albright was not prepared to manage the huge State Department and was better at selling a foreign-relations strategy than forming one.

Senate Armed Forces Committee Chair Sam Nunn, former Senate Democratic Majority Leader George Mitchell, and veteran diplomat Richard Holbrooke were also in the secretary of state sweepstakes. Nunn had never shown any loyalty to Clinton, and Mitchell was perceived to have too many enemies in Washington. Holbrooke had the credentials and media savvy for the post, but he had an attention-getting style that Clinton's National Security Council didn't like.

Albright's close friend, Senator Barbara Mikulski (D-Maryland), continued to persuade Hillary Clinton over veggie-burger lunches. Representative Barbara Kennelly (D-Connecticut) called Vice President Al Gore to promote the

Albright, flanked by Vice President Al Gore and President Clinton, speaks to the press after being nominated as secretary of state.

ambassador for the post. Albright moved very carefully, keeping her distance from the lobbying on her behalf. Then, one December morning when Albright was at her Washington, D.C., home for the weekend, the phone rang. Albright picked it up.

"Hello," she answered.

"Hello," the voice on the other end of the line replied. "This is the president of the United

States. . . . Would you like to be Secretary of State?"
It was a pretty easy answer, Albright recalled. A
reporter later asked whether she had expected
the call. "You never expect anything," she replied.
"I never even thought about the possibility of
being Secretary of State before because who
would have ever thought that a girl who arrived
from Czechoslovakia at age eleven could become
Secretary of State of the most powerful country in
the world. So I am so honored and so proud."

CHAPTER TWO

THE GIRL FROM PRAGUE

Marie Jana Korbel was born on May 15, 1937, in Prague, Czechoslovakia. (She would later adopt her grandmother's name, Madeleine.) Marie was the first child of Josef and Mandula Korbel. She would later have a sister, Katharine (born in 1942), and a brother, John (born in 1947). Her father was an official in the Czech diplomatic service.

Marie was born at a time when her homeland was caught in the midst of political tensions between Nazi Germany and the Western democracies. Czechoslovakia had been created in 1918, when the Versailles Treaty redrew the boundaries of Europe following the defeat of Germany and its allies in World War I. The treaty eliminated the nation of Austria-Hungary, dividing it into three independent countries—Austria, Czechoslovakia, and Hungary. Out of a population of 15 million, the new nation of Czechoslovakia had a significant German-speaking minority of 3 million, most of whom lived in a region along the new Czech-German border called the Sudetenland.

Twenty years later, German chancellor Adolf Hitler used the supposed mistreatment of Germans living in Czechoslovakia as an excuse for demanding the dismemberment of the fragile, young country. At a four-power conference held in Munich, Germany, in September 1938 (when Marie was 16 months old), Hitler, British prime minister Neville Chamberlain, French premier Edouard Daladier, and Italian premier Benito Mussolini reached a peaceful agreement concerning the future of Czechoslovakia. The agreement, known as the Munich Pact, transferred part of the Sudetenland to Germany and guaranteed that the rest of Czechoslovakia's territory would be protected against any further aggression by the Germans. Chamberlain asserted that the Munich Pact would bring "peace in our time."

Just one week after the Munich Pact was approved, however, heavily armed German troops fanned out through the Sudetenland, occupying the hotly disputed border area of Czechoslovakia. U.S. president Franklin D. Roosevelt urged Britain, France, and Italy to do whatever they could to avoid a new war in Europe. The three countries decided to ignore their obligations to come to Czechoslovakia's defense when German troops marched into the parts of the Sudetenland not transferred to Germany in the Munich Pact. On March 15, 1939, the German army arrived triumphantly in the capital city of Prague. Many Czechs who did not claim a German heritage jeered at the soldiers. Others hid in side streets and wept. Czechoslovakia was divided into several regions, all of them obedient to the German dictator.

Once the Germans had occupied their country, the Korbels got their first lesson in tyranny. Marie, who was now called Madeleine (her grandmother's name), was taken to live in London, England, by her parents. "I remember spending huge portions of my life in air-raid shelters singing 'A Hundred Green Bottles Hanging on the Wall,'" Albright later recalled. "I remember when we moved to Walton-on-Thames where they had just invented some kind of a steel table. They said if your house was bombed and you were under the table, you would survive. We had this table, and we ate

> "I remember spending huge portions of my life in air-raid shelters singing 'A Hundred Green Bottles Hanging on the Wall.'"

German troops speed through the streets of Prague,
Czechoslovakia, on March 15, 1939. When Germany
invaded their homeland, the Korbel family
escaped to England.

on the table and we slept under the table and we played around the table."

AFTER THE WAR

The Korbels returned home to Prague in 1945 after the war had ended with the defeat of Germany. Europe had been changed forever, both physically and politically. The United States and the former Soviet Union were the only world powers left intact. While the Western European nations quickly reestablished their democratic governments, the Soviets *annexed* the eastern half of Poland and northeast Prussia. Communist regimes were set up to replace previous governments in the Balkan countries in southeast Europe (Albania, Bulgaria, Greece, Romania, Yugoslavia, Turkey) and in the German territory that the Soviet army occupied. Although Prague had emerged from the war basically intact, the rest of Czechoslovakia fell under the political and cultural domination of the Soviet Union. In 1948, the *communists* took power in Czechoslovakia.

PAST LIVES

Many years after these events, as Madeleine Albright was still settling into her new job as secretary of state, she was hit by a thunderbolt from the past. *Washington Post* reporter Michael Dobbs had researched her life and discovered that her ethnic and religious background was not what she thought it was. Raised as a Roman Catholic, Madeleine has now discovered that her parents were born Jewish and that three of her four grandparents and other close relatives died in Nazi *concentration camps* during World War II. Upon hearing these facts, Albright claimed that both her Jewish origins and the fate of her grandparents had been totally unknown to her and that her now-deceased parents did not tell her how her grandparents died. She never questioned her parents because she had never known her grandparents beyond the age of two. During her childhood, Albright says, "We didn't discuss it. . . . My parents simply said they [her grandparents] had died in the course of the war."

Her parents had fled their native Czechoslovakia twice: first to escape the Nazis and then to escape communism. When the *Holocaust,* the mass slaughter of Jews by the Nazis during World War II, engulfed Europe, the Korbels made a decision to shed their Jewish heritage to protect themselves and their children.

In order to understand their decision, it is necessary to examine Albright's family origins. In the small town of Letohrad (formerly Kysperk, population 3,000), Madeleine's grandfather Arnost Korbel is still remembered as a pleasant and open-minded business leader and humanitarian. The Korbels were one of about a dozen Jewish families in Kysperk. There was no synagogue in the town, and the Korbels, like many Czech Jews, blended into Catholic-dominated Czech society. Arnost and his wife Olga had three children. Madeleine's father, Josef, was the youngest, born in 1909. Josef's birth certificate identifies him as "Jewish and legitimate." This certificate is dated March 1941, when Czechoslovakia's Nazi occupiers required Jewish authorities to provide records of all past Jewish births.

In 1928 the Korbel family moved to Prague, where Arnost became the director of a large company that made building materials. Josef studied law and completed his doctorate in 1933. He joined the Czechoslovak foreign service one year later. By the time Madeleine was born in 1937, Josef Korbel had received his first foreign assignment as press attaché in the Czechoslovakian Embassy in Belgrade, Yugoslavia. Lively and friendly, he quickly charmed the members of the Yugoslav capital's high society.

While the Korbels were in Belgrade, war was threatening their native Czechoslovakia. Under its first president, Tomás Masaryk, the country had become the richest and most democratic nation in Central Europe. By 1938, however, Czechoslovakia was caught in the center of world politics as Adolf Hitler began his plan to expand the German empire.

When England, France, and Italy abandoned Czechoslovakia by signing—and then ignoring—the Munich Pact, the future of Czech independence became uncertain. The turn of events also threatened the Korbel family. The Nazis pressured the Czech government to dismiss all Jewish officials, and Korbel was recalled from Belgrade three months after the Munich Pact. He was assigned to a minor job at the foreign ministry in Prague. German armies marched into the Czech capital on March 15, 1939, seizing control of the country.

The Korbels fled before the Germans completely secured the border, and they headed for Belgrade. It was not safe there either because the Yugoslav government was pro-German. The family went to Greece and from there sailed to England. Madeleine's uncle Jan lived there, having left Czechoslovakia a few months earlier with his family. By September 1939, Europe was at war. London attracted many Czechs who had left their homeland. Tomás Masaryk's successor, Eduard Beneš, had set up a government in exile there that coordinated Czech resistance to the Nazis. Josef Korbel joined the Beneš government in exile and became the head of its information department.

After World War II ended, the Korbels returned to Czechoslovakia. Unlike many European cities, Prague had not been wrecked by the war. Most of Czechoslovakia, however, had been liberated from the Nazis by the Soviet army, which gave the Communist Party a strong position in the new Czech government. In May 1946, the communists received 38 percent of the vote, more than any other political party. Communist Party leader Klement Gottwald became prime minister and Beneš returned to his post as president. As one of Beneš's dependable associates during the war years, Madeleine's father would join the new government.

Around this time, Josef Korbel decided to make his last name sound more Czech. It had been spelled Körbel, with an umlaut on the first syllable. Pronounced *KUR-bel,* it sounded German. He changed it to Korbel—without the umlaut and pronounced with the accent on the second syllable (kor-BEL). *Korbel* is the Czech word for a kind of wooden pitcher used for drinking beer. Either shortly before or during World War II, the Korbels had converted to Roman Catholicism. Madeleine's mother, Mandula, con-

Madeleine Korbel (front) poses with her sister Katharine (back) and a friend in Belgrade, Yugoslavia, in 1946.

fided to an old friend after the war that "to be a Jew was to be constantly threatened by some kind of danger."

In September 1945, Beneš appointed Josef Korbel as ambassador to Yugoslavia. It was an important post because Beneš needed someone whom he could trust in Belgrade to keep a watchful eye on the communist government of Yugoslavia. The 36-year-old diplomat went to Belgrade accompanied by his wife and two young daughters. Madeleine was eight years old, and her sister was three years old. (Her brother, John, had not yet been born.)

Korbel had easy access to Marshal Tito, the leader of the Yugoslav communists, but his democratic views and the years he had spent in London made the Yugoslavs suspicious of him. He found himself in an uncomfortable position: the Yugoslavs were now distrustful of Czechoslovakia, which was caught between the Soviet Union and the Western democracies. The Korbels lived in an apartment in the Czech Embassy, a large, ornate palace. Not wishing their daughter to be exposed to communist propaganda, the Korbels sent Madeleine to boarding school in Switzerland. She would return to Belgrade on school holidays, where she frequently greeted visiting dignitaries. Madeleine often tells reporters, "You know the little girl in the national costume who gives flowers at the airport? I used to do that for a living."

Political events in Prague finally erupted in February 1948. Hundreds of thousands of communist supporters showed up at a rally in Prague's Old Town Square. Communist leaders, who already controlled the city's police force, armed some of the workers and staged a *coup d'etat*. Beneš, exhausted and in poor health, finally agreed that Prime Minister Gottwald could create a new government dominated by the communists.

> "You know the little girl in the national costume who gives flowers at the airport? I used to do that for a living."

Once again, Korbel found himself in a dangerous situation, and he began making plans to leave the country. He found a way out when he was offered the chance to be Czechoslovakia's representative to a special UN commission. Korbel accepted immediately, knowing it would enable him and his family to escape Czechoslovakia.

The Korbel family arrived in the United States at the end of 1948. Applying for political asylum, Josef Korbel wrote: "I cannot . . . return to the communist Czechoslovakia as I would be arrested for my faithful adherence to the ideas of

*A massive May Day parade winds through
Prague in 1948. The Communist Party gained
control of the Czechoslovakian government
that year, forcing the Korbel family to
flee their homeland for a second time.*

democracy." If he had not left Czechoslovakia, he would probably have been prosecuted for his ties to democracy. Many of Korbel's colleagues had already been arrested and put on trial. Some were hanged.

Given the circumstances, it is not surprising that the Korbels shielded their children from the harsh realities that the family had faced. Many

Josef Korbel (seated) discusses business with his colleagues while serving on a special UN Commission to solve an armed conflict between India and Pakistan. In 1948, Korbel applied for political asylum in United States.

first-generation Americans try to forget the events of their lives before coming to the United States. Some call it a personal choice; others consider it a kind of survival instinct. Emigrating to the United States is, in many cases, a conscious decision to escape the past and start a new life. As a result, there are millions of Americans who know very little about what happened to their families before they arrived in the United States. For many years, Madeleine Albright was among them.

As she reflects on it today, Albright expresses no regrets about her own or her parents' choices. "I am very proud of my family, my parents, of what I believe in, what I have gotten—the honor of everything that has happened to me in the United States," she says. In the months ahead, she will have to deal with the new information about her family history.

Madeleine Albright's trip to Prague in July 1997 was her first visit to her birthplace as Secretary of State. The visit began in the fifteenth century Jewish cemetery where her grandparents are

> **"I am very proud of my family, my parents, of what I believe in, what I have gotten—the honor of everything that has happened to me in the United States."**

buried. Her grandparents, Olga and Arnost Korbel, died in concentration camps 55 years earlier.

Standing in the glare of television lights outside the Pinkas Synagogue, Albright tried to hold back tears. She told reporters how she felt at seeing for the very first time the names of her paternal grandparents painted on the wall. On earlier visits, Albright never thought to look for their names, but now, she said, "I know to look for those names and their image will be seared forever on my heart. As I stood look at that . . . wall . . . I felt not only grief for my family . . . but I also thought about my parents . . . about the choice they made."

A professor of Jewish studies at Emory University in Atlanta, Georgia, who has long studied America's conflicted relationship with the Holocaust, has suggested that for Madeleine Albright to question her father's version of her history would be to destroy the hero and role model who most shaped her life.

Asked whether the new evidence about her family's history might change her views of the world, Albright passionately replied, "I have

"I am very proud of the way I lived my life."

always believed the Holocaust to be one of the great horrors of history. . . . I'm very proud of the way I lived my life. . . . I have comported myself in a way that is very much in line with somebody who has known repression and what it's like to be a victim of *totalitarianism.*"

CHAPTER THREE

When she came to the United States at age 11, Madeleine spoke Czech, the family language, as well as French and English. She had picked up French while attending school in Switzerland and English while in England during World War II. Her English was very good, but she spoke with a British accent rather than an American one. From November 1948 until June 1949, Madeleine attended the sixth grade at a public school in Great Neck, New York. By the time she left the Long Island community, Madeleine had begun to adjust to American life. "She consciously tried to become an American and to talk like an American," a classmate recalled. In 1949, Josef Korbel accepted a position teaching international relations at the University of Denver in Colorado, and the family set off in their green Ford to make a new life in the American West.

The Korbel family, pictured here in the 1950s,
moved to Colorado in 1949.

LIKE FATHER, LIKE DAUGHTER

Mandula Korbel was born to a prosperous family, educated in Switzerland, and had always lived a comfortable life. When she married Josef Korbel, she had to adjust to running a household. "Mother used to tell . . . how she had to buy pots and pans but didn't know what to choose because she had never cooked," recalls Albright's brother John, now a Washington, D.C., economist. Mandula, however, quickly adapted to the demands of a diplomat's wife, packing up and moving her family time and again, learning new customs and new languages. For Madeleine Albright, she was a model of resilience.

Albright remembers her father as a strict parent who maintained his European ways. He was a strong influence in her life and gave Madeleine an early start as a diplomat. They used to talk about international relations a lot, the way other families talk about sports or other things around the dinner table. John Korbel recalls, "Madeleine had a special relationship with our father, partly because she followed so closely in his footsteps." The children were expected to be at the dinner table on time. John says the most severe form of punishment was when their father wouldn't talk to them for a week. In 1956, Josef Korbel became the founding dean of the Graduate

> **"Madeleine had a special relationship with our father, partly because she followed so closely in his footsteps." —John Korbel**

School of International Studies at the University of Denver. He wrote many books on world history and foreign affairs, including *Tito's Communism* (1951) and *Twentieth-Century Czechoslovakia* (1976). Madeleine would later tell *Time* reporter Nancy Gibbs, "A great deal of what I did I did because I wanted to be like my father."

Madeleine attended the Kent School for Girls, Denver's most exclusive private high school. In the eighth grade, she won a United Nations contest for being able to name the 51 original UN members. When Madeleine was invited to a ninth grade prom, it started a family feud over whether she would be allowed to ride in the boy's car. Her father offered a compromise: she would ride to the prom with her date, and her father would follow in his car and drive Madeleine home when the dance was over.

COLLEGE DAYS

Madeleine received a scholarship from prestigious Wellesley College in Massachusetts. She majored in political science and journalism, and her

*Madeleine Korbel posed for this photograph
as a student at Wellesley.*

friends called her Maddy. "By then, she was thoroughly American," a Wellesley classmate recalled. "She was a typical '50s college student in Bermuda shorts, shetland sweater and camel hair coat." Most of Madeleine's college friends at Wellesley were Republicans. Madeleine, one of the few

Democrats, campaigned for Adlai Stevenson for president in 1956, but he lost to Dwight Eisenhower. After her sophomore year at Wellesley, Madeleine worked as a summer intern at the *Denver Post*, where she met her future husband, Joseph Medill Patterson Albright. He was the grandson of the founder of the *New York Daily News* and heir apparent to his aunt Alicia Patterson's paper, *Newsday*.

MARRIED LIFE

In 1959, just three days after graduating from Wellesley with a bachelor of arts in political science, Madeleine Korbel married Joseph Albright. The couple moved to Chicago, where Joseph took a job at the *Sun Times*. Madeleine's career in journalism came to a halt when her husband's editor announced that it would be "unprofessional" for a woman to be a reporter. Joseph agreed. It was the late 1950s, and the feminist movement wouldn't come into its own for at least another decade. Madeleine did finally manage to land a job on the public relations staff of the *Encyclopaedia Brittanica* in Chicago. She worked there for a brief time, performing mostly clerical work.

The couple later moved to Long Island, New York, where her husband became city editor of

Madeleine and Joseph Albright share a smile on their wedding day.

Newsday. In 1968, Joseph joined *Newsday*'s Washington bureau, and the family moved to Washington, D.C. Madeleine stayed home to raise their three children—twins Anne and Alice (born 1961) and Katharine (born 1968)—while taking nearly 10 years to complete her PhD in political science at New York City's Columbia University. Albright says the completion of her doctorate degree was the hardest thing she ever did. She would get up at 4:30 A.M. every day, determined to complete her studies. She was doing it not just for herself but to set an example for her daughters. Madeleine wanted to show her children that a person can accomplish anything with determination and hard work.

Anne Albright recalled that "she was always there for us" and added, "What do you do with a mother who is always right? We figured we'd do best to follow her advice." Anne and her sisters used to do their homework together with their mother, who was finishing her doctorate while the girls were in elementary school. At the end of the week, Albright would do the grocery shopping while the girls went horseback riding or took ballet and guitar lessons.

When they were children, the youngest, Katie, wanted to be a firefighter. Anne's twin, Alice, wanted to be a doctor, and Anne Albright wanted to be a baseball pitcher for the New York

Mets. Academic achievement was highly valued, but their mother never told them they should do this or that. The girls were all history majors in college, like their father. They and their parents assumed they would go to graduate school, and they did. Anne and Katie became lawyers, and Alice became a banker. "The one thing [our mother] really wanted to teach us," wrote Anne in a 1997 article in *Newsweek,* "was do your best at your job, no matter what it is. . . . [T]here's no such thing as luck. What you get you work for."

> "The one thing [our mother] really wanted to teach us was do your best at your job, no matter what it is." — Anne Albright

In 1986, Madeleine Albright was the principal speaker at daughter Katie's graduation from the National Cathedral School in Washington, D.C. The ceremony took place in the cathedral itself. In her long, flowing PhD robes, Madeleine strode down the aisle at the head of the procession. It was exciting to see their mother that way, Anne says, and when she remembers that moment and other highlights of her mother's career, she feels tremendously lucky. "As kids," Anne concludes, "we never felt we were being sacrificed for her career. Quite the opposite."

STUDYING HER HOMELAND

Albright's dissertation, or research paper, for her PhD in International Relations focused on the role of the Czechoslovakian press in the short-lived revolution known as the Prague Spring. She based her work on documents and interviews with Czechoslovakian dissidents and perceptively traced the emergence of the forces that led to the end of the old communist regime. In the Spring of 1968, there was a new sense of political freedom in Prague. In the city's central squares, where people had once walked with resigned steps, Czechs were now embracing each other and debating politics in public. Students proclaimed the moderate policies of Communist Party leader Alexander Dubček, who believed in the importance of personal liberty. The most welcome surprise was the return of the newspapers, which were no longer content to reprint Communist Party propaganda.

Dubček's liberal reforms alarmed the powerful leaders in Moscow, who worried that they might spread to other Eastern European countries. When the Soviets failed to convince Dubček to abandon his democratic policies, Soviet troops—equipped with tanks, artillery, and rockets—were dispatched to the Czech border, ready for combat. By August, Soviet tanks had entered the country and were patrolling Prague. Angry Czechs fought back with guns, sticks, even bare hands. They managed to set some of the Soviet tanks and munitions trucks on fire. Explosions rattled the usually quiet Czech capital.

Then, several hundred thousand Soviet troops crossed the border into Czechoslovakia. Weapons and soldiers streamed into Prague in a massive airlift. The skies were filled with the roar of Soviet planes. The Soviets tried to storm the national radio station, and during the attack 30 Czechs were killed and more than 300 were injured. As the station, a Czech announcer urged residents to remain loyal to Dubček. By September, however, the Czech president realized that he was defeated. He shelved democratic reforms and began to toe Moscow's inflexible line, eliminating democratic reformers from the government. Newspapers, radio, and TV were again subject to strict controls. The Soviets withdrew most of their troops, but some remained stationed indefinitely inside Czech borders. On April 17, 1969, Dubček was quietly replaced by Gustáv Husák.

Albright would maintain her ties to the dissidents whom she had interviewed in the 1970s. In 1990, she would serve as Czech president Václav Havel's adviser during his first state visit to the United States. On her first trip back to her native country as a public official in 1996, she flew on Air

In August 1968, a Soviet tank guards the Prague street corner in front of the Czech national radio station. The two burnt-out buses had been used as barricades in a failed attempt to keep the Soviets from seizing the radio station.

Force One with President Clinton. As Albright and Clinton walked down the steps of Air Force One to be greeted by President Havel, she turned to Clinton and said, "It doesn't get much better than this."

ENTERING POLITICS

Albright's political career began in 1972, when she worked on the unsuccessful presidential campaign of Senator Edmund Muskie (D-Maine). In 1976, she became the senator's chief legislative assistant. She found herself jumping from fundraising for her daughters' kindergarten to fundraising for Muskie. When she went to work for the senator, Albright told her daughters that they could call her at the office if anything important came up. When the girls called Muskie's office one day, the receptionist told them that their mother couldn't come to the phone because she was on the floor with the senator. When Albright finally called back, the girls wanted to know what she was doing on the floor with Senator Muskie. She had been with him on the floor of the Senate, of course, but the girls were too young to understand what that meant.

Her next job was in Jimmy Carter's White House, where she handled congressional relations for Zbigniew Brzezinski, her old mentor at

Zbigniew Brzezinski served as national
security adviser to President Jimmy Carter.
He was one of Albright's mentors.

Columbia University. Brzezinski had been the director of the Institute on Communist Affairs at Columbia University when Madeleine was a doctoral student there. Through the years, he advocated a get-tough foreign policy and proved adept at coming up with new policy ideas. In 1977, President Carter named Brzezinski national security adviser. He eagerly presented his ideas to Carter, who called him the best public servant he ever knew. Albright became Brzezinski's choice for congressional liaison between the National Security Council and Congress. In 1978, Albright became a key National Security Council staffer. In his book *Power and Principle,* Brzezinski claims Albright greatly reinforced "the occasionally sputtering overall White House coordination with Congress." In a preserve long dominated by men, Albright emerged as a key Democratic adviser on foreign policy. She left the White House after Carter was defeated in his reelection bid in 1980.

A NEW START

While Albright was becoming a successful career woman, her personal world was falling apart. After 23 years of marriage, her husband fell in love with another woman. Madeleine was devastated. "She thought her marriage, like our parents', would last forever," says her sister, Kathy

Silva. The Albrights divorced in 1982. In addition to the couple's five-bedroom townhouse in Georgetown, she kept their 370-acre farm in Virginia. Joseph Albright later remarried.

Madeleine bounced back from her troubles, channeling her energies into academics. That same year, she became a professor at Georgetown University in Washington, D.C. She taught courses in international affairs, U.S. foreign policy, Russian foreign policy, and Central and Eastern European politics. Her approachability and knack for presenting complicated issues in plain language made her popular in the classroom, and she was voted Best Teacher four times. Dean Peter Keogh, who hired her, observes, "She was like a pied piper. Students flocked to her."

> **"She was like a pied piper. Students flocked to her." —Georgetown dean Peter Keogh**

While teaching at Georgetown, Albright remained involved in Democratic politics. In 1984, she served as foreign-affairs adviser to vice-presidential candidate Geraldine Ferraro. As Democratic presidential candidate Walter Mondale's running mate, Ferraro was the first woman ever selected to run for vice president on a major-party ticket. Albright also advised Governor

*Democrat Geraldine Ferraro ran for vice-president in
1984, the first woman to seek that post in a major
party. Albright served as foreign-affairs adviser
to the vice-presidential candidate.*

Michael Dukakis (D-Massachusetts) when he
unsuccessfully challenged George Bush for the
presidency in 1988. From 1989 to 1992, she served
as president of the Center for National Policy, a
nonprofit research organization that promotes the
study of domestic and international issues.
Throughout the Republican Reagan and Bush

years, hundreds of Democratic party members met at her Georgetown townhouse to discuss current events. These sessions were aimed at laying the groundwork for a Democratic return to the White House.

CHAPTER FOUR

MADAM AMBASSADOR

In January 1993, President Bill Clinton appointed Madeleine Albright as United States permanent representative to the United Nations and made her an officer in his cabinet. As head of the U.S. Mission to the UN, Madeleine Albright worked with her staff of more than 100 people to assure that U.S. interests were reflected in any resolutions, agreements, or treaties negotiated at the UN.

THE UNITED NATIONS

The roots of the United Nations are found in the League of Nations, an international organization that began operations in January 1920. The League's main objective was to maintain peace in the world. It had 42 original members, but the

United States never joined the League because President Woodrow Wilson, its most vocal supporter, couldn't get Senate approval. The League's last assembly was held in its headquarters in Geneva, Switzerland, in April 1946. One of the League's founders closed that assembly with the words, "The League is dead, long live the United Nations!" The efforts of those who had established the League had not been lost because a new international organization, the United Nations, was planned.

On April 25, 1945, men and women of 46 nations had gathered in San Francisco to draft the UN Charter. The document begins by stating the purpose of the organization: "We the peoples of the United Nations determined to save succeeding generations from the scourge of war, which twice in our lifetime has brought untold sorrow to mankind . . . [will] practice tolerance and live together in peace with one another as good neighbors." The original charter also lists the UN's four major aims:

1. to keep the peace
2. to encourage nations to be just in their dealings with each other
3. to promote cooperation between countries
4. to provide a center where all nations can work together in harmony

On October 24, 1945, the United Nations was born, and that date is celebrated as United Nations Day today. The U.S. Senate voted to join the new international organization by a vote of 89-2.

PEACEKEEPING

Peacekeeping remains the most important goal of the United Nations. Madeleine Albright once observed:

> The United Nations performs many important functions, but its most conspicuous role—and the primary reason it was established—is to help nations preserve peace.... There are times when we forget that the United Nations is ... about ... people reaching out to each other.... I have spoken to families uprooted by violence from the homes in which they had lived for generations. I have seen urban neighborhoods constructed out of tin and cardboard ... where nothing grows except the appetites of young children.

Peacekeeping operations are in the hands of three separate agencies: the Security Council (which was viewed as the UN's major peacekeeping agency when the UN Charter was adopted), the General Assembly, and the Office of the Secretary General.

Albright has also noted that another important and basic function of the UN is helping to create a global consensus about what is right and what is wrong. This means setting standards that make international communications and trade easier. "You may think you have never benefited personally from the United Nations," she said, "but if you have ever traveled on an international airline or shipping line or placed a phone call overseas or received mail from outside the country, or been thankful for an accurate weather report—then you have been served directly or indirectly by one part or another of the United Nations system. . . . I have often compared it [the UN] to a business with 185 members of the board, each from a different culture, each with a different philosophy of management; each with unshakable confidence in his or her own opinions; and each with a brother-in-law who is unemployed." Despite the drawbacks of this "business," Albright considers the UN an effective agent for world peace and cooperation.

THE AMBASSADOR'S WORK

Albright's typical day at the UN began at a fast pace. She would often dash from her office for a con-

*Secretary of State Warren Christopher and UN
Ambassador Madeleine Albright attend a
UN General Assembly meeting in 1994.*

sultation with the Security Council, or an aide would grab her for a last-minute meeting. En route to the Secretariat Building, where the Security Council meets, her press secretary might tell her that reporters were waiting to ask her questions. Crossing First Avenue and 45th Street, the two would review what those questions might be and how the ambassador could best answer them. Fielding questions from the press was an important part of Albright's job. The press was always seeking headline news, wanting to know how the United States would make foreign policy decisions on a wide range of issues. The ambassador also attended many official meetings, and some of her top-level conversations even took place in busy hallways.

Albright met with most of the important dignitaries who came to the UN. In this way, she was able to establish a personal connection with world leaders to learn first hand of their goals. She also tried to get to know her staff better by hosting lunches at her official residence. The large, elegant suite of rooms offered spectacular views of the city and served not only as a place to live but also as a place for her to entertain important guests. Diplomats are expected to entertain as part of their job, and sometimes important decisions are made over a relaxed dinner. Albright typically hosted one or more lunches or dinners a week.

The ambassador became known for selecting jewelry—especially the brooches, or pins, that she favors—to make political points. The Iraqi news agency once called her a snake, so she wore a snake brooch when she met Iraqi foreign minister Tariq Aziz. She doubled the effect by wearing a large eagle brooch that has often been part of her outfit, topped with another brooch in the shape of Uncle Sam's hat, done in red, white, and blue.

Albright transformed the job of UN ambassador from passive messenger to power player. In addition to explaining U.S. foreign policy, she helped plot its direction. She was most effective when taking the offensive. Egypt's UN ambassador Nabil Elarby called her a fierce advocate. "She pushes hard," he noted. She once reduced the United States message to Haiti's illegal military government by saying, "You can depart voluntarily and soon, or you can depart involuntarily and soon." Despite her strong stances, she seldom uttered harsh words without first getting an okay from President Clinton.

Some UN diplomats were sensitive to Albright's absence from the so-called party circuit. She pled that she had too little time "to go schmoozing around the halls." The people she worked with appreciated that she was plugged into the White House. Albright's proximity to the president made her a strong force for influencing

*Albright presents a poster
to Burmese political leader
Aung San Suu Kyi
in September 1995.*

the UN's expanding role. "At this stage in world history," Albright says, "practically every foreign policy issue has . . . to do with the United Nations. It puts me in the wonderful position of being there at the takeoff, during flight, and at the landing."

Although New York City was her base, Albright often attended meetings at the White House. She tried to make it to all cabinet and National Security Council meetings because they gave her a chance to have input on the instructions that she had to carry out as ambassador. When she couldn't travel to the nation's capital by plane, train, or car, Albright participated in the meetings through video conferencing. After arriving in Washington, D.C., she usually headed for her office on the sixth floor of the State Department Building. She would meet with her chief of staff, Elaine Shocas, who advised the ambassador on her meetings that day, or she would talk with Secretary of State Warren Christopher before heading to the White House for a meeting of the cabinet or the National Security Council.

In carrying out her role as ambassador, Albright booked a heavy travel schedule and made a special effort to get to know better her essential foreign policy partner, the military. She flew to Mogadishu, the principal port of the African nation of Somalia, when U.S. troops were

Escorted by U.S. troops, Ambassador Albright surveys war-torn Sarajevo, Bosnia, in March 1996.

there on a peacekeeping mission. Driving through the city in an armored personnel carrier, she wore a flak jacket. Albright also toured war-torn Sarajevo, Yugoslavia, wearing a helmet and body armor. She spent many weekends visiting U.S. peacekeeping troops overseas, developing a close relationship with General John Shalikashvali. She even donned battle gear to slog into the fields where the troops were in training. On one occasion, Albright reveled in the cultural diversity of the UN's missions, describing herself as an "American Ambassador in Cambodia being briefed by an Australian commander and flown on a Russian helicopter to review Japanese troops."

A DIFFICULT TASK

One of Albright's most difficult and controversial assignments was engineering the replacement of UN secretary general Boutros Boutros-Ghali. The secretary general serves as the UN's chief administrative officer. Part diplomat, part activist, and part negotiator, the secretary general stands before the world community as the emblem of the UN. The role has expanded over the years with the addition of various political responsibilities to the traditional administrative duties.

Elected in 1992, Boutros-Ghali was the first

African and Arab head of the UN. By 1995, however, the Egyptian diplomat's view of his role as secretary general had become too ambitious for the Clinton Administration's taste. The secretary general clashed with Albright over his insistence that the UN control international forces overseas, and the United States found him unwilling to implement the financial reforms that it wanted. Boutros-Ghali became a symbol of UN mismanagement for critics in the U.S. Congress, who controlled the purse strings for U.S. payments to the UN. Albright and others feared that U.S. influence at the UN was eroding because the country was more than $1 billion behind in paying its UN dues.

The United States got bogged down in what appeared to be an undiplomatic campaign to force Boutros-Ghali out of office. Albright was assigned the task to lead the campaign to deny him a second term. Boutros-Ghali and the U.S. ambassador had gotten along well at first, even dining together frequently. But when it was leaked that the United States would vote against a second term for the secretary general, they found themselves as opponents. Boutros-Ghali was privately offered a deal that would provide him with a graceful exit: he could stay in office for an extra year but then would have to announce his retirement on his 75th birthday. The secretary general declined

In January 1997, Secretary-of-State-elect Albright meets with UN Secretary General Kofi Annan.

the offer, and Albright began working behind the scenes to oust him. Some critics considered her efforts clumsy, but on December 13, 1996, eight days after Clinton nominated Albright as secretary of state, Kofi Annan of Ghana was unanimously elected the new UN secretary general. He took office January 1, 1997.

CHAPTER FIVE

At a news conference on December 5, 1996, President Clinton nominated Madeleine Albright for secretary of state. "I am pleased to announce a new national security team. . . . Each of these individuals has remarkable qualities of intellect, energy, and leadership." Albright responded:

> Mr. President, I am deeply honored. . . . To my daughters, Alice, Katie, and Anne . . . all I can say is that all your lives I've worried about where you were and what you were up to. Now, you will have the chance to worry about me. . . . Because of this nation's kindness we [my family] were granted political asylum. And I have had the opportunity to live my life among the most generous and courageous people on earth . . . [T]he United States is . . . truly the world's indispensable nation.

The president's staff knew that Albright's nomination would be warmly received in the halls of Congress. She had charmed Senator Jesse Helms, who once said, "I've never disagreed with someone so agreeably." Women's groups that had pushed hard for her appointment praised her. In foreign capitals, however, reactions varied. The Israelis cheered. The Russians were worried about her criticism of Serbia during the Bosnian conflict but said that they could do business with her. In Asia, where she had had little experience, leaders greeted the news with caution. Other diplomats questioned whether Albright's charm would work in Arab countries, where attitudes toward women differ. All of them wanted to know more about this Albright woman. Was she the grandmother with the Virginia farm decorated in a cow motif with cow potholders and figurines adorning her kitchen, or was she the slick Washington insider who presided over her own Georgetown political circle?

Critics claimed that Albright was not a strategic thinker. Albright remarked, "I really do think that strategic thinkers who never adjust their strategy or their thinking are not useful. I've tried to have my conceptual ideas but it doesn't do any good to have those if you can't make them happen." Without any kind of grand vision, she seemed very much like Warren Christopher, who had earned a reputation as a master negotiator. On the day of her appointment, she joked about Christopher, "I hope my heels can fill his shoes."

"I hope my heels can fill his shoes."

SENATE CONFIRMATION

Unflappable. Pragmatic. Determined not to waste a moment. These qualities came in handy as Madeleine Albright prepared to become secretary of state. Confirmation hearings took place on Wednesday, January 8, 1997, before the Senate Foreign Relations Committee. Secretary of State Warren Christopher introduced Albright to the committee, the first time an outgoing secretary of state had ever done so. Because Albright and Christopher had been close friends and valued colleagues for 25 years, he said it was a privilege and high honor to introduce her. "I'm sure that her heels will more than adequately fill my well-worn shoes," Christopher said, responding to Albright's metaphor, "I leave the post [as Secretary of State] with great confidence that the new Secretary will serve . . . with great distinction in the years ahead."

Albright went through a long day of hearings on her appointment. While the senators cautioned

Albright that their relations might become more complicated once she is in office, nevertheless the hearing promised rapid and smooth approval by the Republican-dominated Senate, perhaps as early as Inauguration Day. Flanked by her three daughters, Albright immediately showed that she would be more outspoken than the lawyerly Christopher. She impressed the Republican members of the committee with her tough talk. "I am going to tell it like it is, here and when I go abroad," she told the committee. "We must be more than an audience, more even than actors. We must be the authors of the history of our age." At the same time, she warned that the United States should be careful when intervening in conflicts abroad. "We are not a charity or a fire department. We will defend firmly our own vital interests," she concluded.

"I am going to tell it like it is, here and when I go abroad."

The priorities she outlined—the expansion of NATO and a parallel security charter with Russia, the engagement of China in the world of nations, the need to increase the resources available for diplomacy and the importance of the United Nations—varied little from those of her predecessor. She promised complete cooperation with Congress. She told the senators that she

*On January 23, 1997, President Clinton and
Albright's daughters—Alice, Anne, and Katy—
look on as Vice President Gore administers the oath
of office to the new secretary of state.*

would assure that the United States will not hesitate to address frankly the violation of internationally recognized human rights, whether in Cuba or Burma, Belgrade or Beijing.

Committee member Senator Dianne Feinstein (D-California) drew attention to the fact that Albright was breaking the gender barrier in one of the most senior jobs in government. "I feel a great sense of pride" she said. "It is one more door opened. It is one more door that will not be closed." If confirmed, Albright would be the highest ranking woman ever in the U.S. government. (As secretary of state, she would be fourth in line for the presidency if the president became incapacitated. She could never be president, however, because she was not born in the United States.) Afterwards, when well-wishers told Albright, "you sailed through your confirmation hearings," she replied, "Well, I studied. My Christmas vacation was a little like college, when everybody went skiing, and I sat and studied."

On Inauguration Day, Monday, January 20, 1997, only moments before President Clinton arrived for his swearing-in by Chief Justice

> **"It is one more door opened. It is one more door that will not be closed."**
> **—Senator Dianne Feinstein**

William Rehnquist, the Senate confirmed the nomination of Madeleine Albright by an unanimous 99-0 vote. The vote was taken after only a few words and no debate, and many of the senators did not even bother to take off their hats or overcoats. Albright would become the 64th person—and first woman—to serve as secretary of state. After hearing the final tally, she joked, "So who wasn't there?" (One senator was out of the country at the time.) With both Democrats and Republicans supporting her appointment, she observed that the Senate vote "signals a new era of bipartisan foreign policy, and I can't wait to get started." Three days later, Vice President Al Gore swore in Madeleine Korbel Albright as secretary of state.

"I can't wait to get started."

Her predecessor, Warren Christopher, had been somewhat media shy, but Albright, who had edited her college newspaper and had married a journalist, had a good relationship with the press. To introduce herself, Albright held her first press conference on January 24, 1997, at the State Department. She began by talking about three important subjects: people, travel, and priorities. She told her audience that, as a student and teacher of international relations and as UN ambassador for four years, she had gained enormous respect for the people who served the nation in the State Department and represented the United States abroad. She noted that they had worked hard, sacrificed a great deal, and cared deeply about their country.

Today, the State Department maintains missions in almost every nation. A *mission* is a permanent embassy staffed by diplomats and other specialists in foreign relations. Missions typically contain an *embassy* and *consulate*. Each embassy is run by an ambassador, the official representative of the U.S. president in the host country. The ambassador manages a staff of members of the Foreign Service, officials from federal agencies other than the State Department, and citizens of the host countries. Each consulate is run by a consul, the official guardian of the interests and welfare of U.S. citizens in the host country. While ambassadors focus on diplomatic relations, consuls assist U.S. citizens in trouble and deal with visas, business opportunities, trade, and shipping.

THE STATE DEPARTMENT

The State Department stands a block north of the National Mall, near the Lincoln Memorial and the Vietnam Veterans Memorial. To persuade the public of the importance of the State Department, Secretary Warren Christopher established public

A woman makes a call outside of the U.S. embassy in Beijing, China. As secretary of state, Albright is responsible for overseeing the operation of U.S. foreign embassies.

tours of the building, a practice that Albright continues. Monday through Friday, visitors can enter the main lobby to see a colorful array of flags representing the nations with which the United States has diplomatic relations. A special exhibition hall introduces visitors to the history of American diplomacy.

Working directly with the secretary of state are the deputy secretary of state, the counselor (who assists the secretary of state on such special projects as the negotiation of treaties and the preparation of crucial policy alliances), and the undersecretaries for security assistance, global affairs, political affairs, economic affairs, and management. The secretary delegates tasks to several special aides. The State Department communicates and interacts daily with hundreds of other agencies, foreign governments, and international organizations. The department also manages six regional bureaus. One, the Bureau of International Organization Affairs, oversees the U.S. mission to the United Nations in New York City.

NEW OFFICE

In her role as UN ambassador, Albright had become familiar with the ways of the State Department, but she was headed where no woman had gone before her. It amused her that the secretary of state's office, with its own gray marble bathroom, was outfitted, as she put it, "for the boys." There were suit racks and drawers designed to hold men's socks. A reporter asked whether Warren Christopher had given her tips on how to save time with her personal routine. Albright replied, "He can't help me. I wear makeup."

Albright brought her many pictures and awards to adorn her new office, including a basketball signed by the Harlem Globetrotters and a Harlem Globetrotter's jersey. She removed the formal portraits of Dean Acheson and Cyrus Vance, former secretaries of state who symbolized the soft-spoken diplomacy Warren Christopher admired. In their place, she hung three portraits: Thomas Jefferson, Edmund Muskie, and George C. Marshall. Jefferson was the first secretary of state, appointed by President George Washington in 1789. During Jefferson's five-year term as secretary of state, he created a diplomatic service and consular service and assigned all U.S. representatives abroad to one or the other. Muskie had been her boss and one of her mentors.

Her choice of General Marshall gives us the best glimpse into Albright's character. At the end of World War II, the general and diplomat crafted an ambitious economic program called the *Marshall Plan,* which kept half of Europe on the side of democracy. Albright aspires to Marshall's "magic and very American approach," adding that she is "eager to plant the seed of democracy" as he did. She has never forgotten how Soviet dictator Joseph Stalin blocked Czechoslovakia from joining the Marshall Plan.

What came to be known as the Marshall Plan was mainly the handiwork of State Department employees, but it gained its first impetus from a soldier. Marshall served as the army's chief of staff during World War II, and some historians credit him as the architect of the Allied victory. A humble man, he refused to be decorated for military achievements while young soldiers were dying abroad. Marshall served as President Harry S. Truman's secretary of state from 1947 to 1949. During a speech at Harvard University's commencement ceremonies on June 5, 1947, Marshall formally announced the Marshall Plan. He stressed that the initiative for economic recovery in Europe had to come from the European nations themselves. They would be expected to join in a group effort to put the entire continent back on its feet. Congress passed the European Recovery Program in March 1948. Under Marshall's program, the United States provided more than $13 billion in foreign aid. By relieving shortages and boosting morale, the Marshall Plan ensured the rebuilding of Europe and guaranteed the survival

George C. Marshall, pictured here in 1947, served as U.S. secretary of state from 1947 to 1949. He developed the economic plan that helped Europe recover from the ravages of World War II.

of many fragile democracies. For his efforts, George C. Marshall was awarded the Nobel Peace Prize in 1953.

SPREADING HER MESSAGE

After taking office, Secretary Albright's immediate goal was to win friends and support for the State Department. Her first trip was to Capitol Hill, to work with Congress on a bipartisan basis. She also scheduled town meetings and other events around the country so she could explain the who, whats, whens, hows, and whys of U.S. foreign policy. Two weeks into the job, she went to Houston, Texas, determined to take foreign policy straight to the people. She visited Lamar Senior High School, where she delivered on her promise to speak plainly about international affairs. She told a group of about 50 students, "Not only can foreign policy be cool, but it can be awesome."

"Not only can foreign policy be cool, but it can be awesome."

Albright deftly fielded questions on topics from illegal immigration to human rights in China. Sitting in front of a world map, she mentioned that she had failed geography as a girl. "I've tried very hard to make up for that," she said, encouraging the students to meet their own challenges and set high goals.

Albright visited the U.S. Passport Office in downtown Houston and later bought a black cowboy hat, which her diplomatic security service agents carry in a hatbox when she travels. These agents are responsible for carrying all of the secretary of state's personal luggage so that no one can tamper with it. She then delivered a speech at Rice University at the James A. Baker III Institute (Republican Baker had served as secretary of state (1989–92) in the Bush administration). She assured the students, "As Secretary, I will do my best to talk about foreign policy . . . in human terms and in bipartisan terms. I consider this vital because in our democracy we cannot pursue policies abroad . . . not understood and supported here at home." The next morning, she had breakfast with former President George Bush.

> **"I will do my best to talk about foreign policy . . . in human terms"**

NATO SUPPORTER

Albright's maiden voyage—"It's a little hard to be a maiden at this age," the 59-year-old secretary of state quipped—was followed a week later by her first trip abroad. In early February 1997, she boarded a U.S. Air Force jet for an around-the-world trip to Moscow, Paris, Brussels, Rome, London, Bonn, Tokyo, Seoul, and Beijing. One of her goals was to unite NATO's position on its relationship with Russia.

NATO, North Atlantic Treaty Organization, is a powerful military alliance consisting of the United States, Canada, and 14 western European countries. It was established primarily to discourage an attack by the former Soviet Union on the non-communist nations of Western Europe. The breakup of the Soviet Union in 1991 posed a new kind of challenge for NATO. The Soviet Union split into 15 independent nations, most of which rejected communism. Some NATO leaders wanted to offer membership to Poland, Hungary, Ukraine, the Czech Republic, and even Russia. Many people worried that offering membership to former Soviet allies but not to Russia might lead to a dangerous conflict with Russia. To lessen uncertainties about the future of NATO, more than 23 countries, including Russia, joined a program called Partnership for Peace in 1994. Partnership for Peace provides for combined cooperative military planning. Most of the other countries that joined were East European nations.

In the mid-1990s, NATO took military action to help end a civil war in the former Yugoslav republic of Bosnia-Herzegovina. Bosnian Serbs were fighting the government of Bosnia-Herzegovina, and NATO members feared that the war might spread to other countries. NATO's action increased tensions between NATO and Russia, which was an ally of the Serbs. But, by the end of 1995, the Bosnian government and Bosnian Serbs agreed to a peace treaty. UN troops replaced NATO troops as the peacekeeping force in Bosnia.

Madeleine Albright supported U.S. intervention in Bosnia. In her speeches and interviews, she drew on her own familiarity with the Balkan countries and her bitter childhood experiences as a refugee from the conquest of her native Czechoslovakia by two successive *authoritarian* regimes. Albright's background and her consistent, outspoken support for the Bosnian government made her popular among European diplomats.

"NATO is no longer a situation of *you* versus *us*," Albright reassured Russian president Boris Yeltsin, who greeted her warmly in the ornate reception area outside his private office in the Kremlin. Yeltsin spoke without notes and in generalities until reporters were asked to leave the room. Yeltsin then turned to Albright saying, "I've

*On February 21, 1997, Albright greets
Russian president Boris Yeltsin during her
first diplomatic tour of Europe and
Asia as secretary of state.*

heard all about you. Say 'hello' to the American people." Then, at one point, he interrupted his translator, "She understands Russian. Why are you translating? She doesn't need it," he said. Their meeting lasted almost one hour. In addition to speaking some Russian and Polish, Albright speaks Czech and French. Russian foreign minister Yevgeny Primakov called Albright "not just an iron lady, but also a very constructive lady."

Later, using her people-to-people style, Albright took her case for a new, more benign NATO to the Russian people. She tried hard to speak over the heads of the journalists saying, "NATO is not the NATO of the Cold War [a term used to describe post-World War II tensions between the western powers led by the United States and the communist bloc led by the former Soviet Union]. NATO no longer has an enemy to the east. . . . We are on the same side." In Moscow,

"We are on the same side."

Albright was interviewed on NTV, an independent news station. She argued that NATO's expansion was not against Russian interests. "We do know we have a lot of work to do," Albright told the television audience. "But I found a willingness here to get down to work, and that was what I was seeking." On a computer chat on an Internet hookup, she spoke with children at more than 3,000 schools in 49 countries, answering questions both personal and political. Before leaving Russia, Albright also laid the groundwork for the summit meeting between President Clinton and Boris Yeltsin in Helsinki, Finland, in March 1997.

Albright next flew to Paris, where she was greeted by French president Jacques Chirac. He admired and complimented her, kissing her on both cheeks. French foreign minister Herve de Charette outdid his boss, kissing Albright's cheeks five times and calling her "a very great lady from a very great country." Her visit to NATO headquarters in Brussels, Belgium, created considerable excitement. The foreign ministers attending the meeting craned their heads to get a closer look at Albright. Her only female colleague, Turkish foreign minister Tansu Ciler, ran up to Albright and said, "It's the two of us, Madeleine, I'm so excited!"

President Clinton was faced with a difficult question: should NATO be enlarged? He decided that the United States would vote in favor of expansion, pointing out that NATO's time-tested policy of opening the door to new democracies had always kept Europe safe and prosperous. Throughout this difficult decision-making process, the United States's main aim was to ease the Russian government's fear that NATO was trying to take advantage of Russia at a time of weakness. The U.S. position remains that it is more important now to concentrate on the substance of a proposed NATO-Russian charter and not the process of how and when talks with Moscow proceed. Albright has stated that NATO will no doubt go ahead with its expansion despite Russia's objections.

A WOMAN'S WORLD

Once, when Ted Koppel, host of the news show *Nightline,* was addressing Georgetown's School of Foreign Service on the media's role in foreign policy, he had the great misfortune of having Albright in the front row. One student asked why the press had not focused more on the 1984 campaign issues. Koppel responded that he had invited all the presidential candidates to discuss the issues on *Nightline,* but only Democratic vice-presidential candidate Geraldine Ferraro had accepted.

"That's right, and you did a number on her," Albright shot back impulsively. Koppel, not recognizing her, looked quizzically at her.

"Well," he said to Albright, "I have been

accused of being professorial, prosecutorial, and pompous during that interview."

Albright readily agreed. "All of the above. Which leads me to the following question: Do you believe that you . . . were harder on Mrs. Ferraro on foreign policy because she was a woman than you might have been on a man?"

"Yes, we were," Koppel admitted.

The international diplomatic world has been traditionally dominated by men, and women in the U.S. foreign-policy establishment have only been able to rise to such roles as senior advisers at the National Security Council. Albright was able to break through the *glass ceiling* by working twice as hard as many of her male counterparts. "When I work I really work," she told a *New York Times* reporter. "I rub my eyes and my makeup comes off, and I stick pencils in my hair . . .if I wear a red suit and one of the female reporters says I look like a fat little red ball, that's her problem." Even as Albright learned to play hardball in world affairs, she was still teaching her daughters there was nothing wrong with being feminine. Like many women who have worked, she was able to raise her children and keep a home running smoothly.

To help younger women, Albright developed programs at Georgetown University designed to improve the job opportunities for women in international affairs, and as UN ambassador she was active in advancing opportunities for women in national affairs and foreign service. In a recent television interview, she was asked if she thought it was a handicap being a female and trying to deal with the "old boys network" around the world. Albright replied, "I have found it a terrific gender to be."

"I have found it a terrific gender to be."

LOOKING TOWARD THE FUTURE

Throughout her career, Madeleine Albright has been an outspoken refugee from totalitarianism, an unapologetic anticommunist, and staunch supporter of the United Nations. These qualities suggest that she will not often pursue "quiet" diplomacy as secretary of state. Most political observers took her appointment as a sign that Clinton's second term would be a time of greater U.S. assertiveness in foreign affairs.

As she embarked on her role, Madeleine Albright faced many challenges, such as handling the relationships between the United States and the other two major nuclear powers, Russia and China; monitoring the expansion of NATO; and getting Congress to accept the terms of an international chemical weapons treaty. How she manages these difficult issues will help define the presidency of Bill Clinton and determine whether Albright achieves her goal of becoming one of the "authors of the history of our age."

CHRONOLOGY

1937	born May 15, Marie Jana Korbel in Prague, Czechoslovakia (later adopts name Madeleine from her grandmother)
1939	Nazis invade Czechoslovakia; the Korbels flee to London, England
1945	World War II ends; the Korbels return to Prague
1948	communists take power in Czechoslovakia; the Korbel family settles in the United States
1949	the Korbels move to Denver, Colorado
1955	Madeleine Korbel enters Wellesley College in Massachusetts; edits the campus newspaper
1959	graduates from Wellesley College; marries Joseph Medill Patterson Albright
1961	gives birth to twins Alice and Anne

1968	gives birth to daughter Katie; the Albrights move to Washington, D.C.
1976	earns a PhD in International Relations at Columbia University
1976–78	serves as chief legislative assistant to Senator Edmund Muskie (D-Maine)
1978–81	serves as staff member, National Security Council
1982	divorces Joseph Albright after 23 years of marriage
1982–92	works as professor of International Affairs at Georgetown University
1984	serves as foreign policy adviser for Democratic vice-presidential nominee Geraldine Ferraro
1988	serves as chief foreign policy adviser for Democratic presidential candidate Michael Dukakis; becomes key figure in Democratic Party
1989–92	serves as president of the Center for National Policy, a Democratic think tank
1992	President Bill Clinton elected; he nominates Albright for UN post
1993	the Senate confirms Madeleine Albright for US ambassador to the UN
1996	Clinton reelected to second term; he nominates Albright for secretary of state
1997	the Senate unanimously confirms Albright for secretary of state

GLOSSARY

annex to add a region or country to the territory of a larger country

authoritarian favoring concentration of power in a leader who is not constitutionally responsible to the people; blind submission to authority

cabinet the group of government officials—the heads of the executive branch departments and other appointees—that gives advice to the president

communists people who believe in communism, a social and economic system in which property and goods are owned by the government and shared equally by all citizens; communists belong to the Communist Party

concentration camps detention centers used for imprisonment, torture, or execution of political prisoners; during World War II, the Nazi concentration camps were used to provide forced labor and to exterminate an estimated 6 million Jews

confirmation the act of giving consent or approval;

Senate confirmation is required for many high posts in the executive branch

consulate the office of an official appointed by a government to live in a foreign country; this official represents the commercial interests of citizens of that government

coup d'état a sudden, sometimes violent, overthrow of a government

embassy the office of a foreign ambassador

glass ceiling unstated attitudes and/or hidden behaviors within an organization that prevent women or minorities from rising to upper-level positions

Holocaust the mass slaughter of Europeans, especially Jews, by the Nazis during World War II

Marshall Plan a U.S. plan devised by General George C. Marshall to help Europe recover after World War II

mission a permanent *embassy* staffed by diplomats and other specialists in foreign relations

National Security Council the advisory group that makes recommendations to the president on matters involving national security

political asylum protection given to a person who flees his or her homeland to escape danger or persecution

totalitarianism a political regime based on subordination of an individual by the state; a totalitarian state is under the control of an autocratic leader

A NOTE ON SOURCES

I used a wide variety of newspaper and magazine articles as research material for this biography. For Madeleine Albright's own words, I have relied on the following sources: *U.S. Department of State Dispatch*, the *New Republic*, *Time*, *U.S. News and World Report*, *Newsweek*, *People Weekly*, the *Economist*, the *New York Times*. "Remembrance of Things Past," by Michael Dobbs, *The Washington Post Magazine* (February 5, 1997), provided insight into Madeleine Albright's recently discovered Jewish heritage.

Additional quotations have been extracted from transcripts of Albright's first press conference as secretary of state, January 24, 1997; interviews on "Meet the Press" on January 26, 1997, and "Larry King Live" on January 24, 1997. In addition, statements at the confirmation hearing of United States ambassador to the United

Nations before the Senate Foreign Relations Committee, January 21, 1993 and remarks by retiring Secretary of State Warren Christopher preceding the confirmation hearings of Secretary of State-Designate Madeleine Albright, January 8, 1997, were also quoted.

I used Robert Maass's book, *UN Ambassador: A Behind the Scenes Look at Madeleine Albright's World* (New York: Walker, 1995) to gain a clearer glimpse of Albright's tenure as United Nations ambassador. I referred to several books for comments about Albright's career as foreign policy adviser, especially Zbigniew Brzezinski's *Power and Principle* (New York: Farrar, Straus and Giroux, 1985) and Geraldine Ferraro's *My Story* (New York: Bantam, 1985). Another invaluable source was Carl F. Baltz's *The Department of State* (New York: Chelsea House, 1989), which I used for background material on the Marshall Plan and NATO.

Books

Baltz, Carl. *The Department of State*. New York: Chelsea House, 1989.

Dolan, Edward F., and Margaret M. Scariano. *Shaping U.S. Foreign Policy: Profiles of Twelve Secretaries of State*. Danbury, CT: Franklin Watts, 1995.

Lubetkin, Wendy. *George Marshall*. New York: Chelsea House, 1990.

Maass, Robert. *UN Ambassador: A Behind the Scenes Look at Madeleine Albright's World*. New York: Walker, 1995.

Meltzer, Milton. *Never to Forget: The Jews of the Holocaust*. New York: HarperCollins, 1976.

INTERNET SITES

Because of the changeable nature of the Internet, sites appear and disappear very quickly. These resources offered useful information on Madeleine Albright at the time of publication. Internet addresses must be entered with capital and lower-case letters exactly as they appear.

http://secretary.state.gov/
This is the homepage of the secretary of state. It provides a biography of Madeleine Albright and an archive of her speeches and remarks.

secretary@state.gov
The State Department set up this e-mail address so citizens could ask Madeleine Albright questions. Although it's unlikely that Albright herself will answer your e-mail, you're likely to get a response from her State Department staff.

Silva, Katherine Korbel
(sister), 24, *33, 42,* 55–56
Somalia, 67
Soviet Union, 28, 32, 34,
50–51, 84, 91. *See also*
Russia
Stalin, Joseph, 84
State Department, U.S., 11,
20, 67, 79–82, 84, 86
Stevenson, Adlai, 46
Sudetenland, 25–26
Switzerland, 34, 41, 43

Time, 44
Tito, Marshall, 34
Tito's Communism (Korbel),
44
Tokyo, Japan, 88
Truman, Harry S., 84
Turkey, 28
*Twentieth Century Czecho-
slovakia* (Korbel), 44

Ukraine, 88
United Nations, 12, 13, 14,
15, 16–18, *17,* 20, 35, 44,
59–72, 76, 82, 89, 95
Charter, 60
General Assembly,
62–63, *64*
Office of the Secretary
General, 62
Security Council, *17,* 61,
64
University of Denver, 41, 44

Vance, Cyrus, 83

Versailles Treaty, 24

Washington, George, 83
Washington, D.C., 20, 22,
43, 48, 49, 56, 67
Washington Post, 29
Wellesley College, 44, 45, 46
Wilson, Woodrow, 60
World War I, 24
World War II, 25–28, 29,
31–32, 41, 83, 84

Yeltsin, Boris, 89, *90,* 92
Yugoslavia, 28, 30

ABOUT THE AUTHOR

Suzanne Freedman is a former librarian with a penchant for biographies. She has written about varied personalities, from justices of the Supreme Court to primatologist Dian Fossey, boxer Muhammed Ali, and civil rights activist Ida B. Wells-Barnett. *Madeleine Albright: She Speaks for America* is her eighth book.